The Moon Reaches For Me, 7th edition

© 2020, Anna Frazier

All rights reserved. This book or any portion thereof may not be reproduced or used in any manner whatsoever without the author's express written permission, except for the use of quotations in a book review.

Names have been changed to protect the identities of those who have been written of in this publication.

Poems

Published 2020

Edited with Trevor Trosclair

the moon reaches for me

ANNA FRAZIER

collections

Elizabeth Young: The Mind's Mess (2020)

view other collections at
annafrazierpoetry.com.

connect

visit annafrazierpoetry.com to subscribe to email updates on her new collections, view featured poems, and learn more about the author.

dedication

"life is a constant
search for men
and baked goods."
— catherine stauber

note

these books are meant
to be read in order as well
as from left to right.
welcome to a new space.

introduction

Thomas Fairchild:
"Nothing's changed.
He's still David Larrabee.
And you're still
the chauffeur's daughter.
And you're still reaching
for the moon."

Sabrina Fairchild:
"No, Father. The moon's
reaching for me."

— John Williams and
Audrey Hepburn, *Sabrina*,
1954

contents

1   FEAR

    2   LEAVING GIRLHOOD / ITALIAN FLASHCARDS

    16   ADVICE FROM A FOOTNOTE

    23   LIVER

28   ESCAPE

    54   GLASS BUTTERFLY

    77   PLUTO HAS AN ATMOSPHERE SOMETIMES

100   TREASURE

    108   NEEDLEPOINT

    126   WINTER IN MY TELESCOPE

128   REMEMBER / FORGET

    130   MOUNTAIN

    137   OCTOBER TENTH WHILE READING TRANSTRÖMER

154   WONDER

    155   I GO BACK TO NOW

212   JACK / JILL

213   WOOD-PANEL EPIPHANY

226   SAFETY

227   COTTONTAILS IN THE SONORAN

252   LOVE IS A BRIGHT WINTER MORNING

262   STROLLING ALONG THE SEASHORE / 1909

268   REACHING

269   JOURNEY OF ROSES

283   LOVE IN VEIN

286   FOR KOREA

300 – 301   QUESTIONS / ANSWERS

303   THE WINDOW

304   PRAYER

309   A DREAM WHERE THERE IS NO ONE

318   REVIEW

320   ACKNOWLEDGEMENTS

322   NOTES

324   INDEX

fear

leaving girlhood / italian flashcards

fuga (escape) : red cobblestones
pushing my feet into the air, into
l'autobus that caught each midnight
wind.

tesora (treasure) : he held my hand
in evening. i laughed into the empty
streets, but he told me to be quiet,
that i was making a disturbance.
he gave me a rose from the gutter.

paura (fear) : laying curled in the
smallest possible space, fearing my
presence would force the tired man
through another pack of cigarettes.
his red skin splayed across the bed, i

tried not to breath too loud. after
he fell asleep, i used my phone light
to finish my homework.

sicurezza (safety) : opening the
nineteenth wooden door of Via
Aretina at sunrise, sinking into a silk
couch — the door locked, the
mosquitoes buzzing, the quiet
of early morning setting in.

dimenticavo (forgetting) : claude
monet's water lilies wrapping a
florentine journal — thoughts that
i can't decipher anymore. i was
nineteen.

love is not dark

i think there's some small part

of you that likes to get angry

to throw words at me

like rocks off a bridge

just to feel something

but love is not a dark summer night

the truth

the truth about anything

if you close your eyes

it will be over faster

thorns

holding onto something

that keeps hurting you

is like the water in a cabin

that goes from freezing cold

to boiling hot

or

a desert cactus

that sprouts pink

and yellow petals

at night

and in the day

has only thorns

hitting the mark

why can't you just

love me for me

i'm so tired

of being

too much

and

never enough

last minute

why do you think of me last

minute like that one thing

you always go back

into the house for

just before departure

instead of finding me

after a long while

like that thing you lost

and have been looking for

for moons

thin ice

are you going to quit

on me like everybody else

i ask into lips

that say *no*

eyes that say

i'm not sure

and a shaky voice

that is reconsidering

to the independent lover

i could sacrifice a lot of myself

to give you more

to be there more

to love you more

but i am not sure

how to do the opposite

do you really want me

to love you less

my mind

i wonder what it must be like

to be one of those people

that can tell another person

i don't know if i want forever

i don't know if i want

a wooden house or small children

i only know that i love you

my mind doesn't work that way

drowning

you keep pushing my head under

water with your

i could never love you

and

i love you

if i push the water down with

please

will i stay above it

knives for hands

what if you had knives for hands

then i would know

that every time you touch me

i bleed

then i would feel the unsewing

   of my skin-ties

at least if you had knives for hands

i wouldn't be so surprised

every time you hurt me

every time you made my heart cry

   many blood-tears

every time you took what

   you wanted

and shoved the rest aside

something about you

there's something about you

that shuts me up

that makes my self

close every door

and bar it shut

then a million locks

that never let up

there's something about you

that makes me want

to fall open and slam shut

at the same time

like our trust is conditional

or something

sickness

there is something about toxic people

they go within five minutes

from being your best friend

to your enemy

the same way my body does

when i have fallen ill

both are a sign of a sickness inside

advice from a footnote

do not let him slam the book[1] on the bed
so near to your face that it makes a
bluster in your hair when you are
sleeping

do not let him push the book into your
arm as he surges from the sheets
since he doesn't care that your eyes jar
open at his upheaval

do not let him skim you when you are
carefully chosen words on a line

do not let him overlook you like a
footnote when you are a title

do not let him punctuate you when you
are an infinite alphabet

do not let him unnotice you

1. but here i am in the bed with tangled

hair and the closed book pushed into my

arm and his back turned to me with the

light in my eyes as i try to sleep

i can't so i sit up instead

slouched he faces the wall and reads

i am behind him

he turns a crevice

just enough to notice my blankness

he says *what are you thinking*

just to keep me around

to make me think he cares

his too-loud voice jams into my silence

i know he asks me these things

just to say he did

to shut my misery up in a wooden room

you look thoughtful

he says

i am

angel trumpet flower

this isn't fun anymore

the back and forth

the way you get me

right where you want me

and then get angry

when i deviate

from your perfectly laid plans

i'm a butterfly

i go where i want

i fly towards beautiful things

at one time

you were the flower

on which i landed

it took me too long to understand

that you are the kind of flower

that looks alluring

but reveals itself to be

dangerous

poisonous

deadly

your voice

my heart races at your voice

it is like gunshots in my ears

i hear it and i duck

for fear of getting pierced

i examine my own body

looking for a bullet

did you shoot me

was i wounded

— from elizabeth young:

the mind's mess

your voice ii

when i hear your voice

i think of heartbreak

mistakes

and unclean breaks

when i hear your voice

i am filled with war

with hiding and fear

you are a coyote

i am a small hare

i run as fast as i can

but you will always catch me

— from elizabeth young:

the mind's mess

boats in a fog

we are boats in a fog

we see another

we latch on

fearing the let go means oblivion

but at first

my aloneness didn't bother

and i oared through the fog

without care

boredom

i love having this kind of power

some twisted part of me

thinks this is fun

all the energy

i waste on you

maybe it's because

it makes me feel something

liver

silver with relatively low sides
    that flare outwards

a long handle and no lid

i make the mistake of looking

and burn my eyes on the searing pan
    of his body

the sin of laughing too

at the splashes of oil-tongues that
    hop from his mouth

his face grows bigger

a mushroom cloud of steam

rising rising

to caress my face arms skeleton

and while i am warm in him

i still cook

my juices drain

they stick to his edges

the pan drinks my weight in
    pleasure

his high-heat existence crisps
    and browns all my sides

fighting tree

i fell in love with a shadow

a leaning black

of what i thought you were

turns out

where i thought you had two

    loving arms

and a perfectly shaped nose

instead you had just thin branches

and a stump to smell the roses

what the crane saw

young girl walking home roseless

meets boy with no head

    thorny rose-crown gift

her leaving   throws crown

she turns corner   him behind her

meets boy with no fingers

    woven rose-crown gift

her leaving   crown breaks

she turns corner   him behind her

meets boy with no hands

    roses stay in garden

her leaving roseless

she turns corner   him behind her

meets rosebush

    weaves own rose-crown

her leaving crowned

she turns corner

three men come for her

i don't stop

i don't stop thinking about
the ways you've hurt me
the blindness of us both
i don't stop thinking about
you
is what i was going to say
but in a bad way i mean
i don't stop thinking about
how my heart is the sand
and you are the shoreline
coming for me again and again
just to take more of me
for you
all veiled in an ignorance
of not knowing yourself

emotion

both demand to be felt

with love

with pain

you cannot feel any less

you can only feel

the most

escape

screeching halt

he said i love you

when he started us

he said i love you

when he ended us

he said i love you

every moment in between

and then he didn't anymore

atlantic

one mistake

makes us feel

an entire ocean apart

every minute that passes

the ocean between us

takes another bit of sand

of my soul

into its distance

pulling the strands

of my heart

across the world

magic

i will disappear

since i cannot trust in you

to heal my wounds

i will take my fixing

upon myself

and slowly

i will disappear

bear in a trap

so then

how am i

the one caught in the trap

to shed tears for you

who crawled in with me

and if i manage to escape

what obligation

have i towards you

codependence

i'm tired of pulling

the weight of two boats

with you and me in each

even to say the word *boats*

takes it out of me

the pregnant B swells in my gums

popping just enough to allow the O

bulging in my cheek pockets

and the A that bends the O

into something even rounder

to squeeze a tongue-touch around it

the T asks for the S

so it won't be alone

and the weight of the S on the end

of that word burdens my mouth

down to the river

to suck in all the water

to drown me in its consonants

and i lose all my fighting power

the plurality can't be upheld

by my quivering pink arms

let me go

i am fire

when you touch me

i burn you

we are not yin and yang

we are not clouds and rain

all we are are two poles

bending the world in half

to be together

why are we forcing this

want / need

why does sinking

into our tangled past

feel as comfortable

as a winter blanket

as the pillows on your bed

or what i remember

of being in your arms

why did it take so long for me

to become your everything

making up for a night

i'll worry about

missing you later

but for now

i'll worry about

kissing you

before the end

retrograde

although it is bright and warm

i continue to tell myself

do not walk into the fire

chemistry

there's a burning star between us

and we pretend it's not there

sometimes we get too close

and it burns us

sometimes we get too far

and freeze

so let's both touch the fire

and see what happens then

even if we burn up

at least we know we tried

green grass

is it such a crime

to love the burning star

is it so terrible

to crave the thrill

of the uncertain

do you hate this too

and do you love this

like i do

forbidden things

are so much better

vice versa

now i'm just stuck here

with all these feelings

in my mouth

and all this wine

i shouldn't have had

or maybe it's

the other way around

vacation from pain

you know i just want to fall

in love again

that's all i've ever wanted

that's all i'll ever want

we may be dreaming

about different things

but dreaming is better

than bad memories

forbidden

it's four thirteen

and i don't want to close my eyes

i know as soon as i do

i'll have to think about tonight

and all the wonderfully horrible

   things that didn't happen

     but could've

just friends

which is better

with you

i am safe

but away from you

i am capable

"friendship"

i can't sit next to you

if i know that i'm in love

i can't be close to you

if i feel i'm falling

if i see in my eyes

that sparkle in yours

i cannot bear it

i'll have to leave you

red thoughts

am i still in love with you

sometimes these words

    pass briefly through my mind

they threaten to invalidate

    my *progress*

how far i've come from loving you

i turn my eyes and close my ears

because if they were true

i couldn't be here with you

your friend

any longer

protective

i shouldn't

even be dedicating these

cells in my brain

towards you

but you see

that's the problem

i wouldn't want

anybody else

taking care of you

but me

just words

you say you love me

but if you really loved me

you'd stay out

you'd let me heal

love is not suffocating

inconsistent

there are plenty of wonderful people
  in the world
so why did you choose me
to half-want
the moon may shine halfway
but he certainly does not go
chasing after the stars

a cycle

i want you

you don't want me

i leave

you chase fearlessly after me

i turn around to stop you and keep
    walking

you continue in my direction

we both exasperate

i don't do anything halfway

a gift

you wrapped your cowardice
   in friendship
and gave it as a gift
to my surprise
i unwrapped
the leftover scraps
of you not letting go
you can't have it both ways

three pale creatures

i gave you a cactus

to care for and to woo

maybe if you cared for it

you'd care for me too

you left alone the cactus

not thinking of its needs

you went away on holiday

and left it without feed

two fortnights you were gone

from me and the cactus both

there's nothing between us now

the cactus and i have choked

walking away

more than anything
i hate saying goodbye

water

rainstorm after breakup

the sky is crying for me

so i don't have to

glass butterfly : a series

★

stay still

butterflies are glass

still for a moment

but a breath in their direction

   and the paralysis breaks

delicate world

the people on the beach stop walking

tahitian ocean waves quiet themselves

we are a photograph

dust settles on our dark portions

never move

you'll surely puncture this fragile air

★

glass butterflies :

the first time i ever blushed

from happiness

was looking into you

replaying the moment

blue to my brown

smile to smile

now i pause

play back that minute now

i feel my stomach's flight again

   after one whole winter

"chrysalis" is the sound of my love

   for you if she could speak

the voice of wings

that spring from my white arms

& carry me close to you

but the back and forth
your bell jar over me
★   sometimes it lifts only to shade her again
i keep walking
"butterfly-trap butterfly-trap"
a child's lips separate
a song of pleasure and nonsense
someone on the beach points at me
"what black butterfly voiceless
   with its fourth-person narration"[2]
meanwhile, a pitcher plant grows
   beneath the grotto —
encyclopedia : insectivorous plant
   of the tropics that traps insects
   in vase-shaped leaves
trapped insects decompose and are absorbed
   as nutrients by the plant
you — a pitcher plant that lures me
   with your sweet smelling nectar
   into danger poison death

★

and my wings swell with each slog-breath

sliver of decay

she shuts her eyes

yields to the ending

what else is there to do

the people on the beach keep walking

dust settles on the obsidian creature

who swallows

heaves

stay with me

a flash

people say *i loved him so much*

and i can't even say that

because i loved him

but i didn't have time

to love him more than just a bit

he broke my heart before

i could say goodbye

translation

if you were a poem

your consonance would be

on top of your assonance

and your pararhyme

would be mosaic

the structure too experimental

and none of it would be beautiful

how frustrating as a reader

as a lover

monolingual

it is like

i'm monolingual

i can only write in the language of you

how difficult it is to forget

pretty memories

retrospect

i think i figured out

why it felt like all our pieces

suddenly weren't fitting together

after we made the whole puzzle

after we spent months working together

to make all the pieces fit

it is obvious that pieces are missing

and that we never had enough

to begin with

no wonder everything was

so confusing

force

it still hurts

it's going to be

a scar on my heart

for a little while

don't rush me

my pain has no time line

june

june used to be

such a lovely month

you made me hate june

even more than i hate summer

this gave me wrinkles

it's crushing me

and maybe it shouldn't

but it still is

your absence

mentally

physically

is dry ice that burns the skin

even though it's cold

nothing beside your voice

can drag the blushes from

my cheeks

closing

i can barely breathe

being far away from your heart

is suffocating

bruising

tangling

migraining

all of me aching

blur

i've seen too much pain

and i know what's ahead

i can't even see straight

the fear of the future

is too blinding

old hope dies hard

i could cry

a thousand tears for you

but they wouldn't be enough

to fill the canyon

of fantasy that i held for you

silver decay

i wish you never happened

or i'm glad that you did

i wish we hadn't changed

i wish we were kids

take me back to seventeen

to stars and hotels and in between

inside your hug was everything

rewind time to summer weather

i wish we'd known ourselves better

i guess it's better late than never

but i hate to watch

the beautiful thing die

my heart anytime

pieces don't fit together

the right way anymore

there are a bunch of rigid edges

sharp pieces wrong pieces

it hurts the way that a puzzle piece

doesn't fit the same way when

it's put together incorrectly

perspective

then i remember

that there are worse problems than mine

that while i sit peacefully

   on the carpet

writing away about my worries

there are women being swung at

   by angry men

and children watching

ptsd forming

violence devouring any

   holiday gathering

an artist's curse

i always fall in love

with beautiful things

i saw a boy who looked like you

he was lovely

he made my heart beat faster

than rain that patters on concrete

i walked on and began to wonder

if i had only stayed with you

because you were so alluring

and if it was so difficult

to unlove you

simply because of your

irreplaceable beauty

campfire

i sat by a fire

looked into its color

thought

what's the use in how things started

if they were going to end anyway

placeholder

i don't even want
    to love someone new
i just want someone
    to hold me
while i unlove you
i hope it fades quickly

an aching pain

when he is rough with me
i miss your gentle touch
when he is harsh with me
i miss your soft but strong words
when he pushes me too far
i miss the way you listened
when he misunderstands me
i miss the way you were so accepting
   of whatever headspace i occupied
this is the first time
i've missed you
since i've seen you last

pluto has an atmosphere sometimes

the bus vents drip cold and wet onto my just-straightened hair, curling the damp strands. whenever a wheel hits a bump, the bus rattles my bones and its own. it's shaky here, unexpectedly loud, and the hips of my chair poke into me.

this is not some meadow, the middle of an ocean, or a peach sunset that lingers behind buildings. this is the gray silence of passengers.

i blur past all of them riding with me, and my eyes stop on you. you, holding a book. you, hacking at a pear. and between us there hangs pluto.

according to its moons, pluto is paramount. pluto is unable to be ignored by its moons, which circle around it day and night. pluto is between us, the heavy sphere of yesterdays. pluto is the smallest planet in the solar system.

your blue gaze intersects my brown one, then a half-sound from my mouth bubbles up to pop in the air, and slipping off my lap to distract us: my raincoat. i bend forward to retrieve it. the orbit of pluto is chaotic and unpredictable.

i try to catch your eye and do, but not entirely before you look out the window to see wavy bushes and trees. i remember how we used to look through that window and see the squiggles of green and brown and blue.

but then you're hacking at that pear — and do i hear you mumble? and why is there a speed bump, now, right when you're talking? i start up a little from my seat to ask what you said, and in doing so, i lurch towards pluto.

the planet of tension stops me from speaking, and, embarrassed, i sit back into the nineties green. i look out the window at the passing trees and bushes, then look back at you.

your eyes don't search for mine. the metal creature continues to rattle, and the bus vents drip cold onto my straight hair. sunlight on pluto has the same intensity as moonlight on earth.

astronaut

humans cannot live on the moon

what hangs in the air

is heavy and still

there is a moon between us

the pain of not kissing you

weighs on me

pushing against all the stars

as the air dances around us

don't look

don't watch his smile

don't watch the way his hand
   brushes through the blond

and please (to myself)

don't watch the way he finally
   looks at you

i don't care if i hunch
in this moment
if i crush my cartilage because
i can't do anything else
except sink into my seat
except slump
into the confusing memory
of why we aren't together
anymore

black hole

loving someone

who doesn't love you back

is like getting a hole

in your heart

that turns infected

and blackens

nothing helps it and

everything you throw into it

makes the hole bigger

to swallow you

convincing

i go between

you are nothing to me

&

you are everything to me

rosatello

when i talk to you

i think of our last time together

so when i hear your voice

i also crave that sparkling

sweetness

disillusion

i kept trying to tell him

when i'm in a room

i always look at the most

   beautiful thing

and in every room it was him

but his soul certainly was not

as beautiful as i had thought

sorry, no

i saw you and i thought

i am no longer safe

in your arms

yet you ask for my embrace

what am i to do

i don't want it anymore

people are replaceable

i will find another one of you

a bird cannot fly

when it's wings are tied together

love is a choice

love is a choice

& the opposite

but

so suddenly

every flower inside me

that once bloomed for him

died

how do you forgive someone

please forget i exist
i'm begging you to unnotice me
something i never thought i'd wish
    from a boy with green eyes
you've disallowed me to love you
so please allow me to at least
    weave myself into this floor-cloth
    or redden into the brick walls
    around us
may i have no other interaction
    with you
i can't forgive and forget
how do i quietly coexist
or preserve my right to stay silent
and not bother with replying
    to an irrelevant man's colloquialisms
when he says have a good weekend
am i allowed not to speak
may i slip between the books
    into my friday without smiling
    just to make everyone feel okay
    about themselves

i don't feel like browsing the internet
but if i get up from the desk
he'll notice a disturbance
    in our environment and god forbid
he might wish me well
then i'd have to reply

and then jennifer lept from her desk
i thought i might hide in her shadow
but i didn't need to
because you didn't say a word

thank you for letting me slide
    into my afternoon
without calling my curls to turn
    around and utter an insincere goodbye

in the library with the march hare

on this particular day, it is forty-three degrees, and i am sweating.

pyrogens bond to my hypothalamus.

i wind through the university library as Mad Friday pours his tea:

a small cup's contents reflect the March Hare: freckles — dirty specks of absent love — and i add a spoonful of his words — white cubes of confusion.

i remember the cerulean passion of his three a.m. confession.

he undressed me, stamped a curse on my neck, and like the winter wind in north america, retraced his steps to boyhood: "i am nineteen, you are twenty-three," he said. *off with her head!*

beads decorate my forehead. my copper hairs coil. each vertebra on my spine turns away, like god from the son.

for eight fridays i have endured his blasphemous kindness, even as it hurls my valves into palpitating chaos, my mind into a poisonous chroma.

i wonder: is it easier to confess how my red chambers vibrate with each of his appearances? with each absorption of his blushing, sparkful, mud-dusted, terrible, blooming face?

maybe. or maybe i'll delay the comment.

i know — i'll leave it for the ninth friday, when the flashes of our brief affair will send me into Tulgey Wood, and his words, "i'm falling in love with you," will be erased like Mome Raths from my heart.

your heartbreak's shadow

when you're thinking about texting your ex, don't. because after you relive that time on your first date when he got a bloody nose in the middle of your first kiss, and the mood was totally killed when you had to wipe blood off each other while he said "thanks for being cool about this," you'll also relive the way he broke up with you over text while you were at work — how you had to cry in the bookshelves — and when you're finished feeling heart-hurt about the way he took you out on a date and later told you that's how he treats all his friends, you'll realize that good memories and a handful of laughs are not worth the resurrection of your heartbreak's shadow.

to pain-makers

it's not that i wish destruction on you

it's that i wish something horrible

enough happens to you

that you realize the way

you've broken all of us

and never do it again

choose wisely

there is too much said

about selfish people

there are only

those who will give you

everything even when

they have nothing

and

those who will give you

nothing even when

they have everything

freedom

why is leaving you

like pulling two magnets apart

but somehow

after it's over

i feel so wonderful

that i can exhale

without a tightness in my chest

alone

being not next to you

is not my routine

but without you

i can finally breathe

you'll want to return

all of us

we're all going to

find somebody

we're all going to

be safe in the arms

of another person

eventually

wait for he who

lets you fly

rain & i

i love the rain

it makes me feel safer on the inside

and less alone in this string-lit room

it reminds me that

i have all the power in this world

to unlove you

if i really put my mind to it

norms

how do you say

i'm happy without you

without sounding bitter

why do we feel the need

to prove ourselves

to people who don't mind

whether we go without water

dehydration

i went blind

for a second

but i just

kept staring

through the whiteness

until i could

see again

consciousness

the train may have hit

but nothing has died

for once

i can stand on my own

two feet and say

i'm fully alive

repeat

if i know how to do anything

i know how to survive

new years

see not

the many fires

you have walked into

but instead

the many fires

from which you have walked out

and the vast wilderness

from which you have emerged

she knows the truth

you have to hope

you have to listen to your heart

believe her

because every other voice

is just an attempt

to explain

the unsolvable

hometown

i have a lot of memories here

you came and went

so did he

but the common thread is me

library

hopefully one day soon

i'll reach a place in my heart

where i don't look around

in every place i arrive

just to find someone

to hold my attention

or maybe it is the fear

of another pretty face

that will surely make me fall

into another love

that is less than me

needlepoint

i push the silver toothpick until umber knots / become a rabbit. half-moons cross into carnations / with the stitch's breeding passion. the rabbit, now, / with a lignite nose kisses the blossom's yellow center. / his whiskers wear speckles of pollen; a flower gazes / into his freckles, blushing since his nose, so near, / tickles pink her threaded petals. the rabbit's eyes / count dew drops, clear. brown, he brings a rouge / from meadows simply by his gentleness. a blossom / from within me reaches for that love he has, but with / impermanent creatures. i want a human: curious, / permanent, who counts my freckles, ignorant of / pink that dances in my cheeks. i stitch tear drops, / but i can't embroider into life that love.

undercooked egg

there is this feeling

that i am undercooked

like an egg

that must be prepared

to a certain liking

like the whites that

can be seen through

the feeling that i know

i'd be so much better

if i let myself cook

for a little

before jumping off the pan

into the arms of

an irresponsible lover

you know me

i had a dream

that i met myself

befriended myself

and fell in love with myself

how wonderful it was

to be loved by somebody

who knew exactly what i needed

accepting self

sometimes i wish

i was one of those girls

who was happy all the time

and didn't overthink

but then i wouldn't be me

to my little sister

even if no one else

thinks you're beautiful

at least you have to

stained glass

i am

a combination

of all my past lovers

but none of you are the same

pause

if you would stop moving

for just one day

you would remember

how good it feels to be alone

and how bad it feels to be lonely

even the bees are tired

the line

i think what is worse

than death

is the indefinite in-between

how many seconds

does it take to

sift through sand

to find one sparkling grain

debate

i read that victory requires force

to sustain victory

but then what is victory

is victory to move on

and not to feel

or is victory to charge forward

and feel differently

are there things that are impossible

in this world

silver lining

today i am thankful

for not being in love

being in love

is such an exhausting feeling

when they are away from you

it is endless giving

without choice

because the giving

is from the inevitable missing

of the heart

and i've never had a choice in that

broken glasses

i thought

when i had you

when i belonged to you

that i had finally landed

that i was finally

where i wanted to be

only nine days after

i do not belong to you

it is so obvious

that only now am i

exactly where i want to be

neon signs

maraschino cherries

neon signs

and beautiful people

perhaps

one mustn't need

to be in love

to enjoy life

always

i am always in love

with someone

or something

i have lived too much

not to enjoy everything this way

tangerine

i will burn my pain into beauty

the sun shines its light

because it is a ball of flames

nothing is meaningless

it doesn't have

to have a reason

for happening

it doesn't have

to make you better

but it can

it can be purposeless

but it doesn't have to be

meaningless

anything can

happen if you let it

twenties

let's get where we're going

and then find each other

let's not waste them looking

everywhere

this is the time of our lives

head voice

you know what

i just realized

if it's you and me

we don't need anybody else

we have each other

winter in my telescope

concrete thoroughfare, houses
in a row, seventy degrees,
sun hanging low: a peach
in summertime.

alone, i reach up: one hand,
then another, for pink clouds
in their sky-loft; ten empty fingers.
bungalow-roofs frown
against pink clouds that purple,
that bruise, that never stay
for more than a setting sun.

do you think he broke his own heart
when he let himself love me,
even while he looked through
the telescope of his future
and didn't see me there?

surely, now he cries tears
hidden in the sunset: pink clouds
seem to stay longer than us together.

but peaches shrivel, and earth
coldens; bright red berries blush.
snow tops force into colorcut beams;
pink clouds full and fall.

moons mark time without him there.
one hand, then another, holds
onto pink clouds. alone, i beam:
white winter in my telescope.

remember
/ forget

loving again

a heart of ashes

always fears fire

a heart of ashes

understands the destroying power

of fire's fierce flames

a heart of ashes

does not glow again

mine is not a heart of ashes

but a heart of matches

which can glow many times

mountain

suddenly i remembered

how thin he was

and how our bones touched

    when we kissed

how i could never rest on his middle

because he could barely hold himself

    together

i want a mountain

someone who's made of snowflakes

    and thunderstorms

who i can climb and only sometimes

    reach the top

i want to be rained on and swept up

    by a blizzard

and at the end of it all

to land on the rocky tanned skin

    of my lover

things i saw today

1. a brown man that doesn't love me but i don't want him to
2. a heavy-footed man
3. a strange man that never grew up
4. a man on a red telephone
5. a man that looks like my rapist
6. my foot my foot my foot my foot (repetition is what keeps me going and rearranging my contact to blur him so i don't have to see how similar he looks up close)
7. a man with a black umbrella
8. a man with two grocery bags in the middle of the green-lit street
9. a brown man again that doesn't love me

chemistry is dangerous

there is a burning star between us

and

it gets hotter every time

we're together

and

did you feel that

and

i am burned

invitation for epiphany

my mistake is not the apocalypse

i am not ruined

nothing is

but i will not be in the arms of
 another person

if i don't feel safe

for what good could come of that

death by empathy

i always overestimate myself

thinking i can walk into these rivers

    without getting swept under

but my heart is bigger than us both

you are in love with someone

    who doesn't love you back

and that doesn't break you

and spill you

but i am watching someone

    i used to love

be in love with someone

    who doesn't love them back

and it is breaking and spilling me

    for you

reading with a boy

i'd have to be much drunker

to tell you that we aren't correct

and much more sober

to unravel the poems in our hands

you and me don't go together

but how will you ever know

the tension hurts

the air gets drier and the secret

of our inevitable ending

starts to peel off my eyes

you're about to see

a mouth that releases blood

when it speaks

how to be unlonely

why don't i just fall in love

a miscellany of thoughts

will twirl in my head

while a wine swirls in my glass

cherry liquid is a love-potion

every absent bubble

will contribute to my bliss

it's both a great pleasure

and a great danger

to be carried away

so easily

october tenth while reading transtömer

overnight the cold comes,
and moths hitch a ride on favorable winds.
it's 12:04pm, and i wait for the bus.
i read and think of my almost-lover.
my feelings fiber from the words i read:
we do not submit, but want peace.[3]
these lines are my loom.
when his weighted gaze saturates mine,
i wonder if our most arcane thinkings run
together like an estuary. are we like
that silent conversation between
salt and fresh water, or am i threading
together a couple that can never be?
but then, isn't october tenth a fine day
to kiss the neighbor? i have sewn myself
into the air from that ambition, like
mopping oneself into a thoughtcorner. i am
a diseased girl nailed to a dream, stuck
on a rug of almost-decisions.
iphone's marimba knocks me from my
place on the textile.

i cannot ignore what i know —

there is a reason he is my almost-lover

and not a kiss on the second layer

of my lipskin — (i mean by that,

an almost-kiss instead of an actual kiss

that would wear down the first peel

of my lips' pink film.)

but how do you trust a child

to hold a dandelion and not pull away

at its seeds? i read:

if you can play, you won't have to die.[3]

isn't this exactly my heart's gasping attempt

at holding on a little longer

so it won't have to commit the murder

of a boy it never knew?

yarn poem

last night i realized

if you look at somebody with *eyes*

and you still love somebody else

your mind will say *i love you*

because it only knows

those feelings attached

to the love they last came with

your mind will get confused

it will call *like* love

and *love* like

and then it will get tangled

yarn

and this is why

you cannot do anything

with the person you have *eyes* for

until you are finished

being in love

with somebody else

return with roses

the hardest part of all

is to tell a resurfaced lover

that you feel nothing

to tell them you are empty for them

and filled for someone new instead

especially when they say

everything you'd always wanted

to hear

why i disappoint you

i watch a man sleep

there's another out my window

i see all of you

you're everywhere

you're after me in a gentle

    persistence

but what am i to do

with so many men

if none are the right

best friend

i miss you

sometimes you just need someone

to kiss you

i get scared that i'll get hurt again

i fall too fast

i trust too much

too quickly

and too easily

just like you

together we can be

a great pain

re-vision

your socks on my rug

my rug under your pulse

your pulse under my shirt

your shirt on my back

my back in your eyes

my eyes in your hand

your hand in my body pulling out

    what you already know

i could definitely tie my heartstrings

    to yours

cold-blushing

snowflakes are stamped

on the wrinkles in my cheeks

and images of last night

float behind my eyelids

i'm not wearing liner today

just a sweater and mascara

on a black couch

i contemplate the ceiling

with its absence of lights

its indecisive shades

and mirrorless reflection

of last night's decision

then i'm shivering red

loneliness speaks

i remember us inside that restaurant

laughing with the alcohol

talking about basketball

wondering if i would fall for you

the way i never thought

then you targeted my weak spot

do you feel things for me

i think you're lying to me

i think you're dying for me

why aren't you dying for me

i'm your cheerleader

your lipreader

i see that girl

you don't need her

i'm alone

you're alone

we could be together

through all the bad weather

you're looking all around

but i'm so much better

considering

they're not your best friend

unless you're convinced that

sometimes you're in love with them

new expectations

and i am bursting with joyful
    apprehension for my next love
now that i've decided
to expect the impossible
to reach for the moon
to hope for what they say cannot be
and to expect only the best for myself
instead of being comfortable
inside of arms that don't hold me
    tight enough
and adoring a face
that's not nearly beautiful enough
for my artistic mind

darting eyes

a particular customer

is a high paying customer

the way that

a responsible lover

will not settle

either

my eyes bounce

from one heart to another

but i must focus

i saw a boy today

he looked just like you

from five years ago

i remembered

all the faces i've held since then

i remembered everything i've

    settled for since five years ago

it made me so happy to see your

    face again

even if it was on a boy who is

    the same age you were then

and it brought joy to my heart

    to know that there are more

    beautiful faces like yours

    out there somewhere

and that maybe

five years from now

i might be so lucky to hold one

one day is here

seeing someone
so similar to you
made me happy
i knew that one day
you would make me smile
even if it wasn't for a very
   long time

remember / forget

i remember our first date

we ate soup

and you looked at me

like you wanted to fall

in love with me

shrug

we went from *soup?*

to *sorry* and sadness

i've always wanted

to be not so angry at you

i just never could figure out how

to all of you

i say this invisibly

i don't want to change you

i'm sorry i tried

i go back to now

in an office chair

after i remember a poem

i wrote about chopped liver in a pan

    silver with relatively low sides

        that flare outwards

    a long handle and no lid

    i make the mistake of looking

    and burn my eyes on the searing pan

        of his body

    the sin of laughing too

    at the splashes of oil-tongues

        that hop from his mouth

    his face grows bigger

    a mushroom cloud of steam

    rising rising

    to caress my face arms skeleton

    and while i am warm in him

    i still cook

    my juices drain

    they stick to his edges

    the pan drinks my weight in pleasure

      his high-heat existence crisps
         and browns all my sides
i'm grateful i am not a liver anymore
i go back to now
i turn around in my chair
i watch a man
through the awkward tension
of my surprise staring contest
and try to stop thinking
i don't think about my feelings
or his face
i don't even consider
how this makes him feel
after what feels about two minutes
we both smile inevitably

searching

first kisses

are an irreplaceable magic

an unsuppressible craving

just like me

i found you

finally

i've been looking for you

for a long time

you know

being young

kissing you is like snowflakes
    falling in june
velvet rose petals in july
the sound of raindrops absorbing
    into the desert sand

i can never tell you

1. i miss the inside of your hug
   and my lips on your cheek
2. my favorite part of last night
   was just looking at you
3. i'm falling slowly for you
   and it feels safe

it feels nice to be safe

for even one second

you make small sounds

instead of big actions

you move in degrees

instead of fractions

the thrill of fear

on the one hand

why do i do so many things

that scare me

and on the other hand

i must

attaching

i want us to be inseparable

i want us to be laughing forever

i want us to be able to tell everything

i want us to know nothing

could come between us

but it takes time to earn and build

that kind of trust

together and separately

first conversations

last night you said to come to you
    with anything
but right now
where i break down
i don't think you should know
and here i go trusting
someone new again
why does it always feel
like destruction

my own person

thank goodness

we don't have too many memories

thank goodness

we don't have so many

that i can't think

of anything else

when i look at the earth

thank goodness

i fixed myself before you

so i can see

the wildflowers bloom

and the clouds curl

instead of just your face

i am a larger ground to stand on

than the unstable pin-top

that is this new beginning

when i close up

it's not you

it's not you

it's

   not

      you

i scream internally

it's the one before you

my silence whispers

this is what my mouth
can't tell you
when i close up
a sleeping flower

honeymoon

great happiness

reminds me of lingering sadnesses

and i want him

to find me

to come fix me up

to uplift me

like a bouquet from a water-filled vase

but i know he shouldn't

and i shouldn't want him to

this honey moon is too full

its drips overflow and choke me

i throw sadness to the wind

like the moon's shadow

but it returns like the tide

it forms into a bird

landing briefly in my hand

and i can see gorgeous moments

being taken like my smallest bag

    at the train station

what shame accompanies sadness
especially one which grows
   alongside many blooming joys
does every rose have a thorn
   and how do i cut them

blind optimism

what is the cost of hoping

what if i say

it will

it will

instead of

do you think it will

do you think it will

times over

maybe instead of waiting

for it to happen

i'll plan on its occurrence

remove the doubting voice

and continue on

into my own ideal future

with blind optimism

like seven years old

loving a new person

i saw his eyes
glide over my collar bone
his index fingertip
brush my eighth rib
i watched him
trace my scars with his mind
the first boy to ever treat me
like the white rose that i am

i left and sat in my desk chair
viciously flipping through books
of poetry from my shelf
just trying to be okay
with loving a new person

paying attention

you know he's not using you when
he gives your rosy cheeks kisses
he studies your fluttering eyes
    while you sleep
he uses the brief midnight moments
    that the darkness catches him
    awake to kiss your forehead

watch what he does when
he thinks you're not looking
and remember
the way he leaves tells you everything[4]

estuary

maybe it's because

i told the story of my rape

two times this weekend

or because i talked to my ex today

for the first time in two months or

maybe it's because

i stayed up too late

with a boy who finally loved me

the way i'd always needed

to be loved but now

the rivers run down my cheeks

enamored

i write of flowers

that grow in reverse

and butterflies

dying but this

feels the opposite

this is falling for thunder

for the gentle light

that splashes over a city

with a sound that comes

running close after

this is watching a flower's

expedited maturation

or a butterfly reviving herself

two conversations

i miss you

why

    &

i miss you

i miss you too

air castle

fantasies are destructive

i wish a lot of times

that i lived on a pink cloud

with my dog

and you

and everybody i love

but i don't let myself think about it

too much

because i know

i can never have it

take it in

i lay my head on his shoulder

i turned off my phone

i stared off into over-there

what are you doing

he asked

taking in the pink cloud

i replied

between us

but what i've really been trying to say is that

there's a burning star between us

and

did you feel that

and

it gets hotter every time

we're together

and just that i miss you

i really wish you lived next door

aristocats music

i'd rather dance alone with you

than in a drunken jail

in the darkest of the darknesses

where you can see my pale

slowly and quietly

than chaotic bars

they ail

i'd rather be inside your hug

than in endless nights' tales

uncommon

why am i falling in love so quickly

but then

this doesn't feel like

a six dollar souvenir heart

or a sparkler that will burn out

in seconds

tin-can telephone

if i opened my closet

you'd see old telephone wires

all tangled in their own loops

i fight the urge to untangle them

but everyone knows

telephone cords are not likely to come undone

you and me have a tin-can telephone

with a wire too short to tangle

don't stop whispering to the other side

i don't want our little cord to knot itself

resurfaced

he tried to tell me

about he and i from the past

but for some reason

i can't picture kissing anybody else

but you

he and i had our time

it's passed

in rain boots

can you fall in love by accident

the way you step into a puddle

is this a romance where the rules don't apply

where you can fall in love in a week

and marry the next day

love is a choice

but this doesn't feel like one

superlative

i wonder if i tell you

you're beautiful often enough

i wonder if you feel like

a freshly picked daisy

when i hold you

and if you taste

a sparkling waterfall

when i kiss you

i wonder if you notice

when my eyes flash at you

at that burning star between us

i'm curious

do you see the sun

rising and falling

in my smile when you appear

and disappear

i hope you grasp

the ways in which

i adore you

to me you are a white rose

charmed

when i look at you

i see stars

a lot of them

really close together

they're not in your eyes

like a lot of love poems say they are

they're in your face

they're in the way your eyes crinkle

when you laugh

when you smile at me

they fly off your pretty lashes

and make a glow

around your curious fingertips

it's not magic

but something a little bit like it

your voice iii

when i hear your voice

i think of hot chocolate

tiny lights

and sweatshirt-gray

when i hear your voice

i'm filled with velvet night-time

with blushing

and eighty-eight winters

you're a coyote

i'm a small hare

i run as fast as i can

but you will always catch me

sing

when i hear your bending

heaven-soaked song

i think of peace

and of the hops

and hills your voice takes

they're ropes and ribbons

the soundtrack to my universe

my eyes trace each note

on the score like my hand might

run over each bunch and fold

of the silk fabric on an angel's gown

bring me with you

how refreshing

you are a candle

a thing that calms

a thing that brightens

me and the room

a thing that doesn't overpower

a gentle thing

and you smell like flowers

artwork

i was a canvas

upon which he looked

with adoration

and gentleness

i was a masterpiece

his masterpiece

on which he gazed with much pride

a finished work that he kissed

with fondness

i was the girl with the pearl earring

and he was vermeer

a moment which somersaulted

into a constant behavior

forward

is it truly the worst

to daydream

of living so close together

of coming home to you

after a long day

of being a stone's throw away

from your front door

is it so terrible

that i'm excited

for the future

is it such a horrible thing

to be looking forward

to you

rabbit

a boy in india told me

you are a rabbit

he said

when you get close to a rabbit

what does it do

i told him

it runs away

but i'm not a rabbit

and i won't run from you when
    you get close to me

i am water to refresh you

the earth to ground you

the sun to brighten your face

the moon to calm your spirit

i have a home, but yours is nice too

1. your nose touched me
    and your lips touched me
    and your hands touched me
    and i was home
    and that's something
    i could never tell you
    because i know it would scare you
    to think that with you
    i feel at home
    at least
    what i know as home

2. you see

    my home is not always

    quiet peaceful welcoming

    my home doesn't always lack tension

    or fill my soul

    but still

    even when it is not wonderful

    it is still wonderful

    because it is mine

    and it is there

    and it is a part of me

3. i know you don't want to
   be made into a home
   you don't want anyone living inside you
   where frames can be hung
   and fragile things can be broken
   i know you want to be closed
   and alone
   and untrusting
   but please
   let me in

your fears > mine

are you afraid

of monsters because i have one

the dark because i've got that too

my racing mind and my knotted stomach

the same way i am terrified of you

if you had ears

1. i don't feel empty
   when you're not around
   just a little more full
   when you are
2. i don't want you to love
   all my pain away
   just leave it where it is
   and hug me
3. i don't love you more than words
   can describe
   just a little bit
   since it's the beginning

wavelength

i can read his mind

maybe it's his expression

or the degrees up or down

    his smile-corners turn

his eyes catch on mine

he looks at me for just too long

like we both see invisible ink

i wonder for sure what's behind

    his eyes

i know if i stop to think

i can absolutely deduce it

love / other things

i now feel the torture of fire and ice

of standing between them

the way they both bite

the burning and light from two

opposite elements

taking my life and twisting it

into a cyclone of feelings

suspension

there's something inside of me

still damaged

that doesn't understand how to be

    loved the right way

that makes my body physically run

sprint to the end of a bridge

when i hear someone say *i love you*

    for the first time

i think my heart remembers the times

    before this

when people said it and didn't mean it

all the tricks and carnival disasters

    that were in their many hats

and it doesn't understand that

i love you can be safe

it doesn't know that

i love you can be honest

it doesn't know that *i love you*

can be what it is

greenland

but i'm still freezing
from the inside out
my soul shakes like it's chilled
by an arctic wind and it's
the northern lights
inside of me
too many magnetic forces colliding
that all my colors may show

i know you've felt this

last night
we were lovers
but today
we became friends

blond

i am not here

for your sea glass eyes

or your raspberry lips

not for tangled sheets

or hours in your arms

not for five courses

or any gift you give

i am here

for your marbled mind

your infinite heart

and your silver spirit

good for the soul

after the sun sets

these moments pass by my eyes

like petunias caught

in an early winter wind

1. of my eyes closed

your arms around me

and the safety of that

2. i face the ceiling

you think i'm sleeping

you kiss my cheek

3. our eyes are open

our smiles mirror each other

light reaches in

about you

i know you like basketball

a clean house

and things that make sense

i don't know

which season is your favorite

or whether you still think

of your past loves

but i know you are just like me

only more careful

because you have to be

i know you hide

a lot of feelings

maybe for fear of getting hurt

or looking too eager

i know you think about them too

all the things neither of us can say

like a future

the wedding

our children

when i settled

at least now

when i watch hallmark movies

i can picture myself

in someone's arms

that i want to be in

instead of just

somebody's arms

that i can

be in

a gut feeling

you can see forever in someone's eyes

even if they don't say it

even if they can't see it for themselves

even if they're not strong enough to fight
   for it with you

you can always see it in their eyes

because they look at you like they'd never
   want to lose you

as if they glimpse every alternate universe
   behind your iris

it happened with him

it happens with you

hall of mirrors

your eyes say

more than your mouth ever could

more than your words ever will

more than you can even know

in them i see what you cannot say

invisible ink

there are only two things

on the list of things

i could never tell you today

and they are that

i think you love me

and also

that you're too careful to say it

what would you do

if you weren't afraid

the secret i hate keeping

right now

to love you out loud

would be too much

so

to love you well

in the present

is to love you

in silence

repetition

do you think he will

        do you think he will

do you think he will

        do you think he will

the repetition of an anxious mind

quiet thoughts

what i am afraid to say

but i know it will set me free to say it

i want to sit alone

in a room with you

maybe in darkness

beside the christmas lights

on a blue plaid quilt

with our legs crossed

underneath ourselves in silence

so i can hear the noises

your stomach makes

and see the sunrise in your eyes

then maybe after a little while

i will say *hello*

common thread

what has sewn them

all together

love is a choice

attraction is not

relationships take work

and there is no perfect person

possibility

do you choose

to risk everything

in your soul

to feel the darkest

and lightest things

in this world

to see the hidden side

of the sun and

every star

and to feel their fire

within you

isn't that

what life's about

jack / jill

i remember falling in love

i remember it like this

i'm rolling

a little brown-haired girl in a
    gingham dress

down a grassy hill with dirt
    smudged on my white knees

and i'm rolling towards something at
    the bottom

and i don't know what

but i always feel like i'm going too
    fast and i can't stop

i land at some point

and when i land

my legs are sprawled and my hair is
    tossed like spaghetti

but at least i stopped rolling

and i'm looking out into the blue sky

and there's not a single cloud

but it's such a peaceful feeling when
    i finally land

wood-panel epiphany

i see the moon on the water in little slices

and hear fish jumping behind my ears.

there's a well-spoken man leading me across a bridge;

his coat covers my shoulders.

wood panels turn like a stomach under my feet,

and i think, *this doesn't happen to me.*

i don't see moons on the lake, and fish don't jump

behind my ears. men in crowns don't

walk through the wind, coatless, so my shoulders

keep warm from the river breeze. those things

are in movies and fairytales, in children's story books,

and past, rose-colored tales of my ancestors.

but here we are, where wood panels turn

above a moon-sliced water, where fish

hop under my heels, where a crown is placed

at my feet, and i step toward it.

wordless

how do you tell someone

thank you

for falling in love with me

maybe you say

i miss you always

and

you have pretty eyes

and

i've been waiting

so long to be yours

that i'd almost forgotten

how badly i wanted you

the perfect moment

tahitian ocean waves

still themselves

the people on the beach

stop walking

dust settles

on our darkest portions

you looking into me

is glass

we are a photograph

never move

you'll surely

puncture

this fragile air

delicate world

butterflies are glass

they stand still for a moment

but a breath in their direction

and the paralysis breaks

sincerity

glass butterflies

the first time

i ever blushed

from happiness

was looking into you

i can see it

you really love me

day 291

are we too careful

to be careless

and fall for each other irreversibly

i think you love me a lot more

than you originally planned

me too

cord

i go away from you

and it feels like

(a tin-can telephone)

our souls are tied together

and the further away from you i get

the more it seems to pull

with an uncomfortable tension

(a tin-can telephone)

and then you return

another unspeakable

there are many things

i want to be with you

the first

   i cannot say

the second

   your closest friend

the third

   your most brilliant lover

the fourth

   sepia-toned photographs

the last

   someone you no longer know

snow in summer

i like to talk

you know that

but what i like even more

is not to talk

when we're together

it's the sound of snow

so many thoughts

fall through my mind

but when they reach the ground

they like the quiet too much

to make a sound

then i just look at you

three prayers

allow me to love

without limits

with patience and waiting

with silence and forgiveness

and delicate grace

allow me to love

without fear of the future

with space and time

with joy and stability

and respect & regard for the person

allow me to love

without demand

hug without hunger

kiss without thirst

touch without need

without filling my own holes

each night

i have all these thoughts
none of them fit in a poem
but they are here anyway

in the darkness
i haven't been safe with another

&

forever
for once

&

just gratitude
intense gratefulness
that you care for me
with gentleness / respect / loyalty
and hold me like a tea cup

& also

one more thing

that you let me dance

and read poetry

and be so

so silly

thank you for loving me

as i am

cottontails in the sonoran

one spring, a brush wolf trampled desert dust for me. his sound meant war, hiding, and prayer. i was a small hare shadowed by ironwood trees.

i ran as fast as i could, but he always caught me. he let me go each time — i never filled his jaws for blood. autumn brought a final chase: no wolf trampled dune dust for me.

in new snow, i watch a gray, tattered rabbit flee. he digs a hole in the velvet nighttime — he, too, is a small hare burrowed under ironwood trees.

a fresh patch of globemallows pops up beneath some bees. from the nearby burrow, a sun and gray ears rise.

i remember spring — a brush wolf trampled dust for me.

a young coyote rips across our path to brush the tawny ironwood trees. we dive like ribboned snakes into our tunnel. there was a time a wolf pushed against desert dust for me. now, we are small hares covered by one ironwood tree.

dark paradise

the sun pauses beneath us

the earth freezes on its axis

every planet holds its breath

we are all alone with darkness

your eyelashes flutter

and i can feel the smallest wind

blue orbs glow at me

like two moons

your nose touches me

and your hands hold me

and your lips meet mine

and i am home

the unspeakable

like liquid silk

flowing through paris

on a cold raining evening

some shutters fly open

the rain pours harder

i jump out a window

and into your waters

and we swim through paris together

your blue stares up at the rain

and stays still

but my body moves

faster to make yours rush

ripple and roll

i am the swimmer

you are the river

your body is liquid silk

pond visions

bumbling clouds

giant hippos

bloated bees

pulsating billows

i'm under my knees

there's a soft set of tongues

and a hundred pink elephants

loading their guns

to shoot in contagion

lucid colors

a thinning and thickening

gets more extreme

the closer i get

to the shooting machine

the uncontrollable

bumbling clouds

giant hippos

bloated bees

pulsating billows

these are my visions

from the pleasure pond

buttons

leaning my head back

falling off of a roof

into Santorini

floating on top

of the ocean's middle

wrists and ankles

in starfish motion

undulation

the ground breaks

the earth shatters

all the lights shake

my eyes flitter

quickly and without rhythm

as every magic wells within me

buttons tie my outside

to my inside

and a wave of birds

flies out of me

in a splash

aftereffect

what do you see

        somebody that loves me

            (eyelashes)

what do you feel

        your body touching mine

            (freckles)

what else do you feel

        your lips on my cheek

            (cold pressing)

what do you taste

        you kissing me

            (pink bubbles)

i love you

what do you hear

        you loving me

            (white whisper)

what do you smell

        i smell your cologne

            (aqua)

i'm never leaving you

i'm not going anywhere

        (looking)   (trust)

something simple

being with you
is like that feeling
when you finally close your eyes
    after a long day
i'm tired
we stayed awake late last night
but the ten minutes i fell asleep with
    you in my arms were the best ten
    minutes of my day

reading poetry

you unhide a part of me
that i've always stuffed away
we walk through white walls
with small children
wheels click on the floor
and i read to you
and we are stabbed repeatedly
together
with words that cut
through our spines

petrichor ii

i've written them for you too
all the poems that i've written
for the many men
i've written them for you
also
every time i open a page
in my own book
and show you another
it's something i used to feel
that now i feel for you

imaginary

i love you more than

every drop in the ocean

as if it can be measured

love makes us silly

infinite

there is one thing
we will never do
you mentioned it today
go our separate ways
there's a way love
makes a person feel infinite

half

some people love with passion
some people love half-in
half-out
some people just love because they're lonely
and ignore every doubt
but you love with something different
with wind-fire and earth-rain
you love with a force
it seems nothing could restrain
not everybody deserves that

elipses

i knew you loved me
when you spun me around
a hundred times
on the bench swing outside
just to see me laugh

extraneous

i'm not tired of trying
to be what you want
because i already am

pay attention when
you aren't yourself

bursting heart

i could sew my words
into the longest wind
one that wraps three times
around the world
about the baby-blue sweatshirt
that makes his eyes glow
like the sky at twilight
or about the cherries
that stained his cheeks years ago
and how they've been
blushing ever since
or how god wrapped all of him
in freshly picked cotton
so his skin is the velveteen rabbit
i could sew the winds
for each time i knew he loved me
but i could weave the night sky
for each time i knew i loved him

plea

i want to outlove you
i want to make you happier
than you make me
tell me how

be with me

just come be with me

no phone

no movies

no light

no voices

just you and me

i want your eyes looking at me

and your skin

in the dark

and total silence

room

you don't have to look
back at me
i know lots of times you do
and i love that
but right now
you don't have to
look back at me
just let me look at you

no news

i have nothing to write

our loving is as silent as the whales

underwater

as unpredictable as their breaching

as often as their spouting

as glowing as the halo

around the sun

everything else fades

you have to fall for their soul
for the carved out edges
of their heart and the color
of their eyes
you've got to fall for how they leave
how they treat the waiter
how they love their mother
you have to fall for their spirit
because that's the only part
of them that will never die

rose glasses

i think you can love anybody
    into existence
once you fall for their soul
and the carved out edges
    of their heart
their wrinkles and their dark spots
turn more beautiful than
    Cinque Terre
and the places where
there should be less
or *there should be more*
    become just right

evening lamp

if you have to wonder
if they would miss you
that's how you know
they wouldn't
thank god i don't have to wonder

thank goodness for love

thank goodness
i'm not scared without you
thank goodness i can say
you leave
   i'll stay
and thank goodness
i don't ever doubt you
thank goodness
you don't walk away
i could live without you
but i don't want to

the good

i think the thing is
i never realized people exist
that will come into meeting you
with a mindset that says
how will we work together
instead of
will we work out

they are like rainbows
they exist
they're scarce
but as soon as you stop looking
they'll be there
making you believe in the good

love is a bright winter morning

love has been described to us

in fires

and passions

in explosions

and violence

but i think love

is much gentler than that

i think love is blue

and tolerant

that it is has the strength

of an ocean wave

and the peace of its recession

love is not red

or heat

or intensity

love is blue

and cool

and gentle

pond lotus

lucky

understood

i am so accepted

it's a hug from the inside out

and all the space in between

a leaf and a cloud

it feels like many fields

it fills all of the air like lavender

sometimes your love is overwhelming

blue bracelet

a blue bracelet arrived in the mail today

it has the middle of the ocean

the rest of our lives

and a reminder that i tied myself to a person

it has two diamonds and three topazes

and when the sun shakes her scales

the blue shines in my direction

when the dark advances

the gemstones step backward into themselves

which is so very much like me

not always bright or shiny

because it's a lot of energy to sparkle

ten twenty five

sunlight

break of day

spinach sauté

just a tuesday

late night display

making coffee

now it's friday

flat white

caffè latte

yogurt parfait

instant replay

sizzle filet

flower bouquet

little soiree

so far away

stabilizing

there are just certain people
in this world that light me up
that make my eyes turn to sparklers
and without them
i'm sorry
i don't glow in the dark
i am not a crescent moon

somebody

at least i belong to somebody
at least i have a blue bracelet
around my wrist so somebody
would know that i belong
to somebody
if i ever got lost

petrichor

my eyelashes flutter

and i think of holding you in my arms

i tumble into this image

into the thought of kissing you

it's petrichor[5]

a cellous lullaby for my soul

warm

when i think of kissing you
a wave of atlantic water
washes over me
instantly i'm calmed
my spirits are lifted
and my mouth moves itself
into a smile

eyes closed

pink clouds

the middle of the ocean

elizabeth grant

snowflakes

when we smile at the same time

unconditional

both gingham and ink
take decades to fade
and i will never forget
the day i told you
i love you
and nothing you ever do
can change that

strolling along the seashore / 1909

you wouldn't tire from feeling the faucet shoot
a constant stream that wears down gold
*   plating after being left*
*   on for days.*

you wouldn't tire from writing around the frills
of one petunia until you've accounted for
*   the last of its wrinkles*
*   and wax valleys.*

you wouldn't tire from tracing the letter
"k" in cursive form while lead pulls
*   the paper away*
*   from itself.*

you might, however, tire from speaking in a
whisper for several hours, particularly while
*   rain stomps on the grass*
*   and mud and ceiling,*

just the way you'd tire from brushing knots
out of salt-drenched hair after it's dried
    into stretched fingernails
    and earth-crust,

or how you'd tire from a baby pushing
all the uteran seams, or a heart that carries
    unbursted affection
    for a soul inside a person.

cliché

i want to lock you in my heart
    and lose the key
when you find that feeling
how do you have an open hand
it's cliché for a reason

the importance of white teeth

after writing all of these things
    i wonder if you like reading them
i think if i were you
i would very much like to read them
i'm excited for you to see my newly
    whitened teeth
and i wonder if you care about white
    teeth like i do
if i had to make a list of reasons
    why it's good to be alive
i would put pretty white teeth on
    that list
i would also put you on that list
and i thought about saying that
    i might put brown hair on that list
but then i thought that it's not just
    any brown hair that makes life
    worth living
only yours

i let him

let him kiss your nose
let everything happen
sink into that moment with your lover
it won't be forever
no matter what

everything is dying

quit rushing
stop moving
don't be busy
for a moment
and
look into her eyes
instead

they won't always
be there to look into

reaching

journey of roses

from the time i was a seed, i've been cultured to believe there is not a girl like me, for i am sublime. i was under the impression that my traits were an obsession: any man would be a fool to treat me less than prime.

at first, it was entirely true; i found a man who dressed in blue, and, though he crowned me everyday, he didn't have a brain, okay? a handful of white rosebud blooms: my garland-wreath headwear debut. sweet as honey was this boy, his touch gentle as the dove poised, but understanding, he had none, so searching i did go.

next, i found a man with brains who loved me differently: this man loved me here and there, each time giddily. spontane and adventure spilled from his whimsied mind, but underneath that native build, he lacked a soul of any kind. i soon began to understand that he went with the wind, the way he did not crown my head with roses from our garden bed, and how he let those roses die because he feared their thorns' fierce eye. i let the wind take him then, for i needed more than time and again. i wanted a man with courage — a soul — so searching i did go.

turning just around the corner, i stumbled on him there: a man of small but golden stature with roses full and fair. he wove them right into a crown of thorns and thistles, as i stared, that through each other criss'd and cross'd about my curled brown hair. though crown me everyday he did, and a brain he also had, one thing the golden-statured lacked: no compassion — oh, how sad! he loved me hard, not gently like the others, turning my crown to scars.

white petals covered every hallway; with

him, i turned blue and marred. hypnotized by green eyes, light, i couldn't see that every blight unto my crown just brought me down, until i, honest, almost drowned. gasping there with tangled hair, i took a breath of tarnished air and wondered where i'd gone so wrong to fall into the fatal arms of a golden man with such rough hands; i cried until the dawn.

in the morning when i woke, i tried to weave the petals, coax them into that white-rose halo that i'd worn moons ago. the tattered thistles and sharpened thorns wouldn't mend; they were not unworn. i understood what this did mean: i ought to find a new head-ring. for that, i must discover, too, a blushing boy with three things few: a sizeable brain to fathom me, a whimsied soul to fly with me, and gentle hands to comfort me — with these i surely will succeed. but who can locate this rare breed? my hand reached out into space for a mirror, covered in lace: reflecting me, this piece of glass caused my pondering mind to ask, *where will i find such a radiant creature? aren't all men missing a feature?* my lashes drooped and tears rolled down cherry cheeks that wore a frown. *every man that i have met has taken from me; when will i get? is every love just a little war with someone new, and then no more? i think that i will find some thread and make myself a ring for my head. i'll plant the roses in my garden and pick them when the fall leaves darken. then i'll need not any man to make me look and feel so grand.* so push into the ground i did the petals from when i had lived underneath a vicious hand of the last of those untrusty men. this is not a tale, though, of sewing by a garden plough into thorny, flowering plants, my bruises, tears, and sorrow's dance. but instead, it is one of how, no matter how i sunned the bough, in harvest season, i couldn't reason with my roses; they'd all wilted. parched, brown leaves — *i've been tilted! isn't this the story where the princess saves herself? forswear!* nay should you have so assumed this princess resurrects, exhumes. the roses brown, the bushes bare, nothing for herself; nowhere to go or run, to call her home. *maybe i had better roam.* sauntering on, i quit my garden, every tool i left for rotten. *but who will know my royalty if my crown they cannot see? who will love me true, for once, if they lack my roses' touch?* for these questions, i asked the clouds, and in return they sobbed aloud. water poured in a great deluge; the clouds knew not what to do. *neither i, nor i, nor i,* said each townsperson that i queried speech. then all over, i started to worry. sitting down, my dress so dirty, a tiny heap i formed upon the green, green grass i'd been walking on. *how have i been so mistreated? thrown around and even beated, not considered, not esteemed — why is everyone so mean? i thought i had the blooming flower every man sought out to bower. what a large miscalculation. no man seeks this ratted carnation for any reason better than hats or some ornate, hand-sewn doormat. endearing men with my lace, my beauty and my endless grace, the joy i supply in buckets leaves me empty while they drink of it.* i could go on, but you understand the misconceptions of my headband. here i had such faith in the goodness of humanity. but after being jostled 'round, what faith had i to be found by someone with each fine feature, and then, looking up, i saw a creature.

pale like me, his oceanous eyes poured their pools onto my guise, and feigned to wash my dress 'til white shown into the dim twilight. barely could i see right then, as i was still a bowing wren, but as i rose to dawn his smile, sensed not i one ounce of guile. gracing lightly my barren head, he lowered a rosey crown, undead. descending to the grass with me, he questioned if my hand would be better interlocked with his, but Hesitance didn't miss her queue to enter this new space; she sat near as my heart raced. he and i commenced conversation; my ears felt a satiation with his voice, a calming presence; so pleased was i with his essence. our words were like a hummingbird that grew just as the moon upwards went higher, higher, higher still until no more it could be willed, although i truly wished it would — i'd found someone i thought i never could. the sounds between us tied like ribbon, knotting every inch; we seemed to make each other sparkle — i needed, quick, a pinch! he showed his brain by listening; he offered well-advice. he veiled not his soul of lot: it seemed of a great price. and as we know, when he bestowed the crown of roses, he proposed the gentlest of hands that curled right around my skin, like pearl.

so...

no mystery may it be that i have chased him happily across the world with roses glowing atop my head and buckets flowing toward me with many gifts. this is what i think love is: simple and not dangerous, warm and welcoming at dusk, kind and gentle in the morning, listening and ever-growing.

now, i've planted in my garden, which i'll pick when fall leaves darken, a white rose tree with shining leaves greener than the emerald beams, so i can weave him with my gloves a crown of honor and true love.

sent away

this is not a love poem
but this is what happened

on january fourteenth
a tuesday
instead of any of the other days
i was sitting in a red leather chair
at a nail shop with my mother
and my telephone opened its eyes

a message :
just like that my world crashes
i might be leaving for korea
i'm so sorry

the room spun
like a russian dancer

korea

korea populates my brain cells
it rests on my neurons
(a bear in winter)
it surrounds their atmosphere
(magnets)
korea korea
in the layer between my bone-skull
   and my pink lobes
there is korea
korea makes my brain swell
i can't think of anything
nothing but korea
it's a crown i don't want to wear
a robe not comforting to me

korea is everywhere : in the tv
in these poems and the news
i grieve the loss of my lover
a dark deer from near the train tracks
of *some place like chicago*

i grieve the loss of my lover

who stands near a *k*

that has never been more aggressive

my right eye hasn't twitched this
   way

since my first understanding of
   death

dust storm

korea is not everywhere today
it's more underneath
    than everywhere
a dust that fogs every thought
    now settled
(the great depression)

the same way diamonds
    and migraines are made
is depression made
    that way too
with compression
that was a question

i got a depression once
but i wasn't sure if it was because
somebody died
or because the weight of waiting
    for her to die
compressed me so much that
i myself settled like the oklahoma
    dust storm

he and i were driving through

oklahoma

last weekend

he gave me a white rock from

    a souvenir gas station

that said *oklahoma* in monotype

    cursiva

will that turn to dust too

love in vein

your legs top a chair by a tree-filled window. oval, olive, oakish slips of leaves plead with your brown eyes to read their color. but Doubt clouds your vision, like water from the sky, so you can only see the sky's light and not its color from your place above ground.

your eyes pull through the glass window the nearly black and white leaves. Doubt-turned-adrenalin has blurried all their color, but slowly, the leaf-tops reflect a faint, blue sky — puffing, blue caterpillars of light that might slip off and drop to the ground.

you project time through your mind-window. your dizzied brain leaves the chair to jump in a pool of Inquiry, your least favorite color. your backward eyes look into a Western sky for something besides short, black light. you find a dark, Korean mountain, a new ground:

you pick up withered Oxalis Violacea* and say through your window, *why do they droop, the once-strong leaves? their faces are hidden by violet color, and they've stopped pulling down the sky with their stems. why hasn't the sky pulled them up with its light?* interrupting your daydream, two voices drag you to the first ground.

your eyes turn forward, then down. children look toward the window and shoot their fingers up at the tree leaves. they censure the leaves' undersides and frown at the color. but you know they can't see the leaf-tops with caterpillar-sky. maybe you're underneath a light too. maybe there are caterpillars puffing above your ground;

*Oxalis Violacea is a Korean wildflower whose name means "love in vein"

maybe there are grounds above you. wind ripples the window. your eyes pull at the sky. they drag past the leaves. blue velvet grabs your sight, a single color shouting with its brightness from a blank sky. you remember the surrendering flowers, and Doubt, and a ceiling light from above the window becomes your ground.

you glance at the children through the window, how they can't see the color, and you wonder what's above your sky.

for korea

i hope your fingers are ice and warm (eucalyptus), / since only healing hands can carry my one singing thing, / that your air is crystal and your water fills throats (golden hour), / because between the deserts, on top of the pear fields, / underneath my roses (dried), we sweat with our eyelids, / he and i, and we scratch our own wrists, ears, with telephones, / and we wish down the well for a better connection (tin cans) — / so, korea, i hope you make his cheeks glow, so the me listening / on the other end will brighten (edison), which will make / our blossom spike over the tall pacific, where when / he gets back, we will arch together as two orchids pearling / (purpling) just for each other, and then there's the green / to follow; that's why i hope your people are kind, / ever pushing into his shy heart, that you'll take care of him / when i can't. my arms don't reach across the aurora (thin).

long distance poetry notebook

facetime

waiting by the phone

the absence of a body

wearing his sweatshirt

flipping the personalized calendar

miscommunication

giving encouragement

looking to the future

changing schedules

coordinating times to talk

feeling lonely

wondering if i can do it

knowing i have no other choice

playing with the dog a lot more

sewing

watching netflix

staying up all night

missing my best friend

being patient

prayer

dark pink

maybe i'll write a poem

about just your lips

and then i sat down

to remember their lines

and i couldn't

inspiration

my rhymes and letters

like you better

they've left me altogether

they've followed you by canoe

resulting in poems few

with you here

my words appear

but when you're far

i'm no composer

please come here

i need you closer

screensaver

i thought about changing my screensaver
to a picture of you and me
i thought of the pictures we've saved
    together
they're few and far between
two months near and two months far
make our photo album small
since we hadn't time enough
in nearness to capture memories
there's a most convincing picture
the one of you kissing my cheek
from the night we crashed a quinceañera
and you told me on top of popping fish
    you loved me
for some reason that picture hurts
    to think about
to look at it doesn't feel like the way we
    are now
when you're too far to kiss my cheek
my favorite picture now a pain

resonance

people ask if we're still together
they haven't seen you in my pictures
i tell them if they squint their eyes
they can make you out
right behind my eyelids

tired of living without you

i just want to hear you sleeping
to hear you turning
while i am weeping
all i want : to hear you breathing
to have a moment
while i'm weeping
where i am watching
and you are sleeping
and you can't see that i am weeping

closet

the light is broken

he told me he wants to go hiking

   in the appalachian mountains

   when he gets back

i said

do you want me to come with you

he said he hadn't thought it through yet

for the next sixteen months

i'll wonder if that meant

no

when you don't call

when did the well with no bottom
become a well with no bottom
maybe it was the small drips
over a long time that were once
a tap and became a pounding
as the clock passed by five everyday
maybe the drips knocked the bottom out
and i fell down with it

three days without speaking

every cell in my body fights
my virgin instincts to trust a boy
that hasn't called
but last time he didn't call
he told me not to assume the worst
except the problem is
every boy that's ever told me
they loved me despite them
not showing up has ended
up not having as big a heart as me
and now
here's another boy telling me to trust him
like it's something i should just do
and not a process i have to work through
i'm working on accepting
and looking at facts
like
accepting he's not available
instead of thinking he forgot me
and looking at his wanting to call me
instead of simply his lack of a call
this is new

we're not in a famine

nothing is enough for my heart
like she's starving all the time
why won't she quiet down
herself being filled with kindnesses
    from many countries
she wants more
she's greedy
and i don't know how to satisfy her
my stomach hurts
she's eaten a part of it
so the moths float up and down
    from my stomach to her
brushing their moth-dust onto her
    ventricles and drying her out
she destroys herself

why is it so painful
to have something to say
and not be able to say it

summer petunia

i want his words to be enough for me

i want it to land when he says *i love you*

i want peace to adhere when i hear him

    tell me *everything will be okay*

and i want him to feel like he's filled me

and like i couldn't ever want more

i want to be a desert cactus that stores up

its water instead of a summer petunia

    that loses it all by noon

reinforcement

    he loves me

             he loves me ~~not~~

    he loves me

             he loves me ~~not~~

    he loves me

             he loves me ~~not~~

record

can we get back to being children again
can we table our disagreements
problems
anger
for long enough to remember
why we're in love
how much we laugh
and how silly the world is
when we're together
i need to hear the music
in order to keep dancing

questions

do you still love me across the ocean

are we growing apart over the phone

do i still mean everything to you when we don't speak

do you want out after a fight

am i a bother when i break down

could you live without me a drunk thought

why aren't we connecting well at an italian restaurant

do you get tired of my issues on a thursday

would you change something about me if you could in the middle of the night

if you really knew me would you still want me when i'm alone

answers

i laugh you smile you stuff your face into a pillow / every day isn't anything new we have nothing to say you call anyway you like to hear me talk about nothing / i ask if you get tired of me you say *no i like you* / everything goes wrong on thursdays i call you listen i hear *it will all be okay* / it's silent for minutes we stare at each other you tell me i look beautiful you ask if i know kangaroos can't jump backwards / it's five o'clock you call me exhausted all you get out of your mouth is *i love you* but you still do / i write you sleep the internet fuzzes i keep you here / bad news i cry you stare at your ceiling we listen to white noise so we can be miserable together / double migraine panic on repeat i think we're over but we never are you won't let us be / i fall asleep you wait an hour you say *goodnight* even though i can't hear you / you say you wish you could give me more of yourself that's so silly you give me so much every day

treasure

usually people say *i don't deserve you*
which shouldn't be true
so i started deciding whether they
    deserve me instead
and i found only one

(i can't believe i have someone that
doesn't use me)

the window

i am a person

i am a person who lost strength in a
   moment

i am the one that a person
   hears but doesn't understand

i'm the one curled up in a corner
   looking out at all the furrowed brows

i'm the one looking through a window
   to see your glowy eyes look back at me

i'm a face who sees your funny face
   and forgets my aloneness

a face that follows your shifting gaze onto
   a checkered white butterfly

you and i chase the pearlish blur
   with our laughing eyes

&

with hands that could hold an elephant-
   -heart

you catch its flying spots

you open your hands to me and it folds

you're like light on a shadow

you take me away

prayer

behind his constant smile
i know something's missing
displacement knocked joy out like a
    shattered mirror that's got bits of silver
    still shining in the corners and
like one of those jars that pours and pours
there's a hole in the middle of his heart
    where peace should be
because he's given it all to me
there are cracks between kindness and
    patience where they've grown and
    pushed into each other
and where gentleness has inflated
it's found its sides to be ripped
like a shirt that's too small

dear god
please put the pieces of his heart back
    where they belong
so he can be whole again

patience

i will wait for you

i will wait for you to come through

your own darkness

the same way i waited for

my father

my mother

and myself

because that's what love is

reel

i wish i could replay the moment
you saw me after not
for such a long time
i wish i could pause my life
and play that minute over and over
just to feel in my stomach
the butterflies
that flew out of your arms
and carried me closer to you

what i hold onto

i remember how he was when he
> was here

we were laughing

we were talking

we were in the middle of the ocean

drinking balloons

climbing up the sides of upsidedown
> mountains

we were watching each other
> watching the tv

slicing avocados and falling asleep
> with a dog in between us

now instead of reaching across a dog

we're reaching across the pacific

it's blurry to see him through
> the water sometimes

but our memories are crystal clear

"you look beautiful"

i'm not sure if he was taught to say it
    or if it's just how he feels
but it reminds me what i could've
    been hearing
all this time
all these other men were just
    white noise

a dream where there is no one

i'm running on cement squares toward you. the neighborhood bounces in my eyes. numbers and american flags hop down and up with me, and one-story houses crouch in the shade like ground squirrels. music makes my feet blot like ink drops splashing into solid stomps.

the heavy thumps distract me from how *tu me manques* every hour of the year, but a yellow image propels me forward: i will finally have you; i will breathe again.

i stop where the sidewalk ends, against a wall of oak leaves and twisted tree trunks. looking around and removing the music from my ears, i enter a humid silence. i stand heaving and beaming outside of a house. slowly, my head tilts to see if you're behind a corner. there is no one. only a used house that has packed up to leave. its steps are bare, and the lights have gone out.

a cold realization flies over the wall of trees, crashing into me like the north wind, and i remember. you're not here, and won't be for months. you're not on holiday, and you haven't come to see me just for one day. you're trapped in another country.

my extreme heart deflates, an unblown sail. cool air suddenly forces my hopes into a downburst. a gradual rain begins throwing spots and making noise. turning around myself, i search an empty neighborhood for someone to tell that you're gone, that i was running toward a wish with dream eyes.

the tree-wall begins to stretch and wash away as i question how my imagination eclipsed my conscious mind. my eyes stay open, and my mouth is drawn continuously downward until it's stretched from my face to the concrete.

i wake. a fan sways like an empty swing above me, and that instant of almost greeting you in warm pleasure dissolves. my windows glow soft-white. red patches form on my arm, and i shiver. i understand my world. *i am not running. you are not here.*

intangible

at the beginning
i remember hurting so much
because i couldn't be in your arms
but now i don't remember either
   of those feelings
maybe because i don't want to
maybe it would hurt too much
   to feel something in a memory
   that you can't hold onto

parking lot

i was on my way to target to buy a blow drier
and i had to pull into a parking lot
because thinking about how
someone is willing to work with me
instead of waiting to see if i fail
how scary the world is
and how
every time i talk to him
i feel less afraid to face it
was too overwhelming to continue driving

he told me

we are where the atlantic

and pacific ocean meet

we are made of the same material

and are similar to many

we mix by nature

but at the same time

we have a distinct line

where people can tell we are different

a new way to thank you

i want a new way to thank you
the old one's lost its luster
i love you is a reminder
but sometimes i still wonder

if there's a new way to thank you
for sewing my stray tatters
for making my thoughts into flour
then bread that we share together

i know no new way to thank you
for loving me across borders
for lifting my head when showers
heavy my heart with thunder

i know you don't ask for thank you's
for inviting me into your house
or gifting me red flowers
a woman couldn't want more

but this is my thank you
a letter to my lover

review

leave a review of this collection on annafrazierpoetry.com in the "contact" section.

reviews help the author's collection to be viewable by a wider audience, so others can share the experience that you have just had reading the collection.

acknowledgements

trevor — thank you for constantly supporting my feelings and ideas. you get me, and i'm lucky to have a friend like you.

brandon — you made me feel beautiful always, and you constantly impressed me. thank you for giving me everything you had. you were the moon; thank you for reaching for me.

notes

Geoffrey Bunting created the beautiful cover art.

1. see page 17

2. Julie Carr, *

3. Tomas Tranströmer, *The Half-Finished Heaven*

4. Rupi Kaur, *Milk and Honey*

5. Keaton Hanson, "Petrichor"

6. *Strolling Along The Seashore*, Joaquín Sorolla y Bastida, 1909

index

2	LEAVING GIRLHOOD / ITALIAN FLASHCARDS
4	LOVE IS NOT DARK
5	THE TRUTH
6	THORNS
7	HITTING THE MARK
8	LAST MINUTE
9	THIN ICE
10	TO THE INDEPENDENT LOVER
11	MY MIND
12	DROWNING
13	KNIVES FOR HANDS
14	SOMETHING ABOUT YOU
15	SICKNESS
16	ADVICE FROM A FOOTNOTE
18	ANGEL TRUMPET FLOWER
19	YOUR VOICE
20	YOUR VOICE II
21	BOATS IN A FOG

22	BOREDOM
23	LIVER
24	FIGHTING TREE
25	WHAT THE CRANE SAW
26	I DON'T STOP
27	EMOTION
29	SCREECHING HALT
30	ATLANTIC
31	MAGIC
32	BEAR IN A TRAP
33	CODEPENDENCE
34	LET ME GO
35	WANT / NEED
36	MAKING UP FOR A NIGHT
37	RETROGRADE
38	CHEMISTRY
39	GREEN GRASS
40	VICE VERSA
41	VACATION FROM PAIN
42	FORBIDDEN

43	JUST FRIENDS
44	"FRIENDSHIP"
45	RED THOUGHTS
46	PROTECTIVE
47	JUST WORDS
48	INCONSISTENT
49	A CYCLE
50	A GIFT
51	THREE PALE CREATURES
52	WALKING AWAY
53	WATER
54	GLASS BUTTERFLY
60	A FLASH
61	TRANSLATION
62	MONOLINGUAL
63	RETROSPECT
64	FORCE
65	JUNE
66	THIS GAVE ME WRINKLES
67	CLOSING

68	BLUR
69	OLD HOPE DIES HARD
70	SILVER DECAY
71	MY HEART ANYTIME
72	PERSPECTIVE
73	AN ARTIST'S CURSE
74	CAMPFIRE
75	PLACEHOLDER
76	AN ACHING PAIN
77	PLUTO HAS AN ATMOSPHERE SOMETIMES
80	ASTRONAUT
81	DON'T LOOK
82	BLACK HOLE
83	CONVINCING
84	ROSATELLO
85	DISILLUSION
86	SORRY, NO
87	LOVE IS A CHOICE
88	HOW DO YOU FORGIVE SOMEONE
90	IN THE LIBRARY WITH THE MARCH HARE

92	YOUR HEARTBREAK'S SHADOW
93	TO PAIN-MAKERS
94	CHOOSE WISELY
95	FREEDOM
96	ALONE
97	YOU'LL WANT TO RETURN
98	RAIN & I
99	NORMS
101	DEHYDRATION
102	CONSCIOUSNESS
103	REPEAT
104	NEW YEARS
105	SHE KNOWS THE TRUTH
106	HOMETOWN
107	LIBRARY
108	NEEDLEPOINT
109	UNDERCOOKED EGG
110	YOU KNOW ME
111	ACCEPTING SELF
112	TO MY LITTLE SISTER

113	STAINED GLASS
114	PAUSE
115	THE LINE
116	DEBATE
117	SILVER LINING
118	BROKEN GLASSES
119	NEON SIGNS
120	ALWAYS
121	TANGERINE
123	NOTHING IS MEANINGLESS
124	TWENTIES
125	HEAD VOICE
126	WINTER IN MY TELESCOPE
129	LOVING AGAIN
130	MOUNTAIN
131	THINGS I SAW TODAY
132	CHEMISTRY IS DANGEROUS
133	INVITATION FOR EPIPHANY
134	DEATH BY EMPATHY
135	READING WITH A BOY

136	HOW TO BE UNLONELY
137	OCTOBER TENTH WHILE READING TRANSTRÖMER
139	YARN POEM
140	RETURN WITH ROSES
141	WHY I DISAPPOINT YOU
142	BEST FRIEND
143	RE-VISION
144	COLD-BLUSHING
145	LONELINESS SPEAKS
146	CONSIDERING
147	NEW EXPECTATIONS
148	DARTING EYES
149	I SAW A BOY TODAY
150	ONE DAY IS HERE
151	REMEMBER / FORGET
152	SHRUG
153	TO ALL OF YOU
155	I GO BACK TO NOW
157	SEARCHING
158	JUST LIKE ME

159	BEING YOUNG
160	I CAN NEVER TELL YOU
161	THE THRILL OF FEAR
162	ATTACHING
163	FIRST CONVERSATIONS
164	MY OWN PERSON
165	WHEN I CLOSE UP
166	HONEYMOON
168	BLIND OPTIMISM
169	LOVING A NEW PERSON
170	PAYING ATTENTION
171	ESTUARY
172	ENAMORED
173	TWO CONVERSATIONS
174	AIR CASTLE
175	TAKE IT IN
176	BETWEEN US
177	ARISTOCATS MUSIC
178	UNCOMMON
179	TIN-CAN TELEPHONE

180	RESURFACED
181	IN RAIN BOOTS
182	SUPERLATIVE
183	CHARMED
184	YOUR VOICE III
185	SING
186	HOW REFRESHING
187	ARTWORK
188	FORWARD
189	RABBIT
190	I HAVE A HOME, BUT YOURS IS NICE TOO
193	YOUR FEARS > MINE
194	IF YOU HAD EARS
195	WAVELENGTH
196	LOVE / OTHER THINGS
197	SUSPENSION
198	GREENLAND
199	I KNOW YOU'VE FELT THIS
200	BLOND
201	GOOD FOR THE SOUL

202	ABOUT YOU
203	WHEN I SETTLED
204	A GUT FEELING
205	HALL OF MIRRORS
206	INVISIBLE INK
207	THE SECRET I HATE KEEPING
208	REPETITION
209	QUIET THOUGHTS
210	COMMON THREAD
211	POSSIBILITY
212	JACK / JILL
213	WOOD-PANEL EPIPHANY
215	WORDLESS
216	THE PERFECT MOMENT
217	DELICATE WORLD
218	SINCERITY
219	DAY 291
220	CORD
221	ANOTHER UNSPEAKABLE
222	SNOW IN SUMMER

223	THREE PRAYERS
224	EACH NIGHT
227	COTTONTAILS IN THE SONORAN
229	DARK PARADISE
230	THE UNSPEAKABLE
231	POND VISIONS
232	BUTTONS
233	AFTEREFFECT
234	SOMETHING SIMPLE
235	READING POETRY
236	PETRICHOR II
237	IMAGINARY
238	INFINITE
239	HALF
240	ELIPSES
241	EXTRANEOUS
242	BURSTING HEART
243	PLEA
244	BE WITH ME
245	ROOM

246	NO NEWS
247	EVERYTHING ELSE FADES
248	ROSE GLASSES
249	EVENING LAMP
250	THANK GOODNESS FOR LOVE
251	THE GOOD
252	LOVE IS A BRIGHT WINTER MORNING
253	POND LOTUS
254	BLUE BRACELET
255	TEN TWENTY FIVE
256	STABILIZING
257	SOMEBODY
258	PETRICHOR
259	WARM
260	EYES CLOSED
261	UNCONDITIONAL
262	STROLLING ALONG THE SEASHORE / 1909
264	CLICHÉ
265	THE IMPORTANCE OF WHITE TEETH
266	I LET HIM

267	EVERYTHING IS DYING
269	JOURNEY OF ROSES
278	SENT AWAY
279	KOREA
281	DUST STORM
283	LOVE IN VEIN
286	FOR KOREA
287	LONG DISTANCE POETRY NOTEBOOK
288	DARK PINK
289	INSPIRATION
290	SCREENSAVER
291	RESONANCE
292	TIRED OF LIVING WITHOUT YOU
293	CLOSET
294	WHEN YOU DON'T CALL
295	THREE DAYS WITHOUT SPEAKING
296	WE'RE NOT IN A FAMINE
297	SUMMER PETUNIA
298	REINFORCEMENT
299	RECORD

300	QUESTIONS
301	ANSWERS
302	TREASURE
303	THE WINDOW
304	PRAYER
305	PATIENCE
306	REEL
307	WHAT I HOLD ONTO
308	"YOU LOOK BEAUTIFUL"
309	A DREAM WHERE THERE IS NO ONE
312	INTANGIBLE
313	PARKING LOT
314	HE TOLD ME
315	A NEW WAY TO THANK YOU

www.ingramcontent.com/pod-product-compliance
Lightning Source LLC
Chambersburg PA
CBHW020900080526
44589CB00011B/380